PHONICS READERS
Steck-Vaughn
Plus™

Wishing for Fishing

Written by Laura Lionello
Illustrated by Kathryn Capri

STECK-VAUGHN
COMPANY

A Division of Harcourt Brace & Company

June 17

Dear Tanya,

Early today we left on our camping trip. We'll be at Lapping Lake for two whole weeks. I sure hope I catch some fish!

Will write again soon,

Amy

We're on our way!

Dear Tanya,

   We got to Lapping Lake today. I
helped Dad set up our tent. Then Simon
went fishing. I skipped rocks across
the water. I watched Simon catch a huge
fish. It was a bass. I can't wait to catch
one, too.

              More to come,

              Amy

Look where we camped!

Dear Tanya,

   Today we went hiking in the hills. I jumped over tree trunks and crawled under low branches. We hiked and ran all day. Simon walked right through poison ivy. He is still itching and scratching. I still have not gone fishing.

        Later,

        Amy

Hiking is the best!

Dear Tanya,

Mom and I went horseback riding. My horse was named Brownie. I picked some green grass and fed it to him. When we finished, it was time for supper. Dad said it was too late to go fishing today.

Till next time,

Amy

This is Brownie. He nibbles my hair!

June 24

Dear Tanya,

We went swimming all day today. We floated on inner tubes, too. I even learned to dive. Then it started to rain. No fishing today!

Love,

Amy

Can you believe this lake?

Dear Tanya,

Today Dad and I rowed all the way across the lake. We saw a huge bear. It started running toward us. We rowed as fast as we could. We almost tipped the boat over! After that I was too tired to go fishing.

Miss you,

Amy

Check out the bear!

Dear Tanya,

   Dad cooked hot dogs and roasted marshmallows over a fire. We sang songs and played guessing games. Then Mom told spooky stories. Simon and I screamed. I was too scared to think about fishing.

   Can't wait to see you,

   Amy

A campfire looks so pretty at night!

Dear Tanya,

    Today we packed up and headed home. Who knows? Maybe NEXT year I will get to do some fishing.

        See you soon!

        Amy